Handmade Houses

Steven Paul Whitsitt & Tina Skinner

Schiffer Publishing Ltd

4880 Lower Valley Road Atglen, Pennsylvania 19310

Other Schiffer Books by Steven Paul Whitsitt & Tina Skinner
The Kitchen Guide. Laura Jensen & photographer Steven P. Whitsitt. ISBN: 9780764328893. $29.95
Built to Last: A Showcase of Concrete Homes. Tina Skinner. ISBN: 0764316176. $29.95
Garden Projects for the Backyard Carpenter. Tina Skinner. ISBN: 0764312340. $19.95
Log Home Lifestyles. Tina Skinner. ISBN: 0764317539. $34.95
Radford's Artistic Homes. Tina Skinner. ISBN: 0764314556. $19.95

Other Schiffer Books on Related Subjects
Award-winning Green Roof Designs: Green Roofs for Healthy Cities. Steven W. Peck. ISBN: 9780764330223. $39.99
Houseboats: Aquatic Architecture of Sausalito. Kathy Shaffer AIA. ISBN: 9780764327223. $39.95
Old Stained Glass for the Home: A Guide for Collectors and Designers. Douglas Congdon-Martin. ISBN: 0764316842. $29.95
The Passive Solar Primer: Sustainable Architecture. David Wright, AIA. ISBN: 9780764330704. $29.99
Stained Glass Windows and Doors: Antique Gems for Today's Homes. Douglas Congdon-Martin. ISBN: 0764322761. $39.95

Designed by "Sue"
Type set in Bernhard Modern BT/Zurich BT

ISBN: 978-0-7643-3203-6
Printed in China

Schiffer Books are available at special discounts for bulk purchases for sales promotions or premiums. Special editions, including personalized covers, corporate imprints, and excerpts can be created in large quantities for special needs. For more information contact the publisher:

Published by Schiffer Publishing Ltd.
4880 Lower Valley Road
Atglen, PA 19310
Phone: (610) 593-1777; Fax: (610) 593-2002
E-mail: Info@schifferbooks.com

For the largest selection of fine reference books on this and related subjects, please visit our web site at **www.schifferbooks.com**
We are always looking for people to write books on new and related subjects. If you have an idea for a book please contact us at the above address.

This book may be purchased from the publisher.
Include $5.00 for shipping.
Please try your bookstore first.
You may write for a free catalog.

In Europe, Schiffer books are distributed by
Bushwood Books
6 Marksbury Ave.
Kew Gardens
Surrey TW9 4JF England
Phone: 44 (0) 20 8392-8585; Fax: 44 (0) 20 8392-9876
E-mail: info@bushwoodbooks.co.uk
Website: www.bushwoodbooks.co.uk
Free postage in the U.K., Europe; air mail at cost.

Preface

More than a decade ago, I had the pleasure of meeting David Ballantine during a weekend jaunt to Woodstock, New York. We were introduced with little more than a "this is someone you'd enjoy" by my new boss and Publisher, Peter Schiffer. I did enjoy meeting him, and I enjoyed a gift he left me with, *Woodstock Handmade Houses*, a book he'd co-authored with Robert Haney. It meant nothing to me in my burgeoning publishing career, but served as a simple joy whenever I needed to reflect on architecture that was beautiful without costing a buck. This was really important for my personal reality checks as I delved further and further into the world of half-million dollar kitchens and multi-million dollar homes. That sage boss and publisher said lots of things to me that helped shape my career. He also funded trips to Portland, Oregon, where, by happy circumstance I stumbled upon my first book by Art Boericke and Barry Shapiro. I've since collected all three of their inspiring books: *Handmade Houses: A Guide to the Wood Butcher's Art*; *Handmade Homes: The Natural Way to Build Houses*; and *The Craftsman Builder*. I'm not alone in my passion for these books, though I admit I'm among a scarce breed in conservative Chester County, Pennsylvania.

That's why I needed photographer Steve Whitsitt to walk through my door. Steve works in the same circles as I – memorializing high-end kitchens for designers around the United States that only millionaires could hope to own. He creates shiny visages of these culinary palaces that make the rest of us feel like our kitchens are overweight and have pimples. However, within five minutes of our meeting he'd let down the veil and stated his true purpose, which is to contribute more to the world. Thus our mutual ambition was launched to help celebrated beauty without bankrolls.

Once again, that sage and wonderful boss comes into the picture (as do bankrolls). Peter Schiffer gave us the opportunity, and the means, to visit incredible homes and memorialize the self-taught, self-made, creative-spirit — to celebrate homes of unforgettable artisans.

Many thanks to those homeowners, to Peter Schiffer, to Art Boericke, Barry Shapiro, and David Ballantine, for inspiring a spirit we hope to rekindle for home-dwellers yearning to build free. And thank you, Steve, for walking through that door and daring to be different!

Tina Skinner

P.S.: Art and Barry, if you're still out there, please call!

Photographer's Note

Looking back at the images represented in this book brings to mind two revelatory experiences that I had over the course of creating it. The first is the transition from shooting film to shooting 100 percent digital. The first photos of Rainbow's lovely little home in Virginia, and Maurine's funky little artists cottage in California were shot mostly on film in the 4 x 5, and 120 formats. I had resisted transitioning from film to digital for two major reasons. First the overall quality, sharpness, and color representation that I was accustomed to seeing in the transparencies that I was shooting was superior to what I saw with digital, particularly in the world of architectural photography where I do most of my work. The second reason was that while I saw the quality of digital images improve, I still didn't see the lens coverage at the wide angle range that is needed for architectural photos. Additionally, in the interest of full disclosure, I saw the very high-end digital systems as cost prohibitive for me.

In early 2008, the foundations of the photography world were mildly shaken with the news that Polaroid Inc. would cease manufacturing all of their instant films. These had been integral to my work for checking composition and lighting since my career began in the late 1980s. Now I would have no choice, I would have to dive head first into digital.

After exhaustive research, I finally settled on Nikon's D3 body and a 24mm tilt/shift lens, both products which had been introduced only months earlier. I had been using a Nikon D200 for detail shots for a while, so I wasn't completely unfamiliar with shooting in the digital format. The learning curve was steepened somewhat by the fact that I had to make the transition without skipping a beat. I had just barely taken the new camera out of the box when I had to start shooting professional jobs with it.

One of my first discoveries was that the actual shooting process became significantly quicker; I could set up a shot in half the time it would take with the old system. This was offset somewhat by the added time at the computer, editing and tweaking the photos in Adobe Photoshop. But the speed of the shooting allowed me more time to explore and find more interesting images to create in these extraordinary homes.

I was freed up in another way too. In my everyday work shooting residential architecture and interior design, I am constrained to the mission of accomplishing my client's goals, interpreting their vision, often within a pretty tight budget. This isn't a bad thing; it is just an aspect of my work. But between the combination of the new freedom of the digital system, and the amazing creativity that I discovered in the homes that we visited for this project, and their amazing owners, I was injected with a new level of excitement. These photos were not work at all, but represent me having an absolute blast discovering just how much fun people could have by stepping outside of convention and letting their own needs and tastes dictate the environment that they create for themselves.

This project was truly a joy, all of the homeowners were fascinating individuals, and I enjoyed spending time with each of them. I am honored that they allowed Tina and me into their homes and so generously shared their stories and insights with us.

Steven Paul Whitsitt, October 2008

Contents

Sculptural Village of Eliphante

The trunk-like entrance of Eliphante inspired its name. The first of Michael Kahn's buildings, seven years in the making. He crafted it from salvaged glass, ferro cement, and every imaginable kind of throwaway he could find. The "nostrils" of the trunk are divided by driftwood, which piles up in abundance along a nearby creek each spring.

Eliphante is an enormous, delightful, otherworldly monument to art and the human desire to build. Lucky circumstances and inexhaustible energy converged in the desert south of Sedona, Arizona. Years later Leda Livant is in awe as she looks around the four-acre art installation she created with her husband, Michael Kahn.

It started in 1979 when the pair were traveling in truck and tent to move to the Southwest from Provincetown, MA. Actually, it started before they met, in 1970.

"Michael had an experience in 1969, just a year before we met. He was doing charcoal representation figure drawings, but he felt his hand was being guided. Before he knew it, he was doing paintings that totally transformed his life, and mine."

Before long, they were off on a life journey together to pursue art, and wound up in Arizona.

"We accidentally met the people who owned the land. They wanted someone to act as caretakers," Leda recalls. "Local people thought it was a national park, and they were coming in and trashing the place."

The couple were poor as could be, with only a thought toward having the freedom to create art. "There was an artesian well and electricity here, but we didn't have the money to tap into them," Leda relates. Years later she does enjoy a computer, a DVD player, and other modern amenities.

"My family told me it was crazy, but now they want to be here, and visit regularly."

It took eight years for Michael to complete the first building on the site. A friend dubbed it Eliphante, noting that its tunnel entrance resembled a pachyderm's trunk. "By the time Eliphante was done, we knew it was a work of art and too important to live in." After building Eliphante, they spent seven years in "Leda's Winter Palace" before moving to the Hippodome.

Thus began a series of buildings and spaces that came to define what feels like an outer space village and garden.

Mesquite driftwood comes down with the creek's floodwaters each spring, and a nearby wash is full of interesting rocks. "Michael just played with everything." Eliphante is full of rocks impossibly balanced and driftwood awash in color.

Michael died in 2007 of Pick's Disease, a progressive brain disorder similar to Alzheimer's that robs the sufferer of his ability to speak. However, "Michael painted right up to the end, painting six hours a day when he could no longer express himself verbally. And he walked every day. He was outside all day," Leda relates.

His legacy is now an Arizona state tourist attraction, featured in state tourism brochures and written about in *Arizona Highways Monthly Magazine* (April 2008) and *The New York Times*. Friends Matt Leo and Susan Drury have helped to create and update a website, and Blue Feather Tours (928-963-0271) schedules small groups to visit the place and help raise money for its upkeep.

"This was not built for practicality. It's not a very practical place. It's a work of art." It is also in need of a new caretaker, and Leda is searching for a home for Michael's more important paintings to keep them away from the constant encroachments of desert weather and critters.

"Michael was the driving force. He had to paint every day. And he had to create every day, with whatever came his way. There's a dry wash near here about a quarter mile long. All the flat rocks here came from the dry wash in a burlap sack on Michael's back, or in my arms. It was like building the pyramids. I look now and I say 'Did we really do this?' We did it!"

A framed portrait of Leda and Michael hangs on a wall Michael painted. They are shown in context on their Astro-turfed art installation. Leda left an average middle-class life after falling in love with Michael, an artist who made her realize that there was another way to pursue life.

The inside of Eliphante has served as art gallery and music hall for those lucky enough to visit.

Salvaged auto glass was "stained" by epoxying colored glass to it. "He played with glass and rock the way he did with paint." Every flat stone in the riverfront Eliphante complex was carried to the site from a nearby ravine where Michael went walking almost every day, bringing treasure back in a burlap sack slung across his back.

Not all of the color on the sculpted concrete and stone floor comes from filtered sunlight – Michael painted on everything. Rocks and trees throughout the grounds bear the marks of his brush.

Flat, level surfaces are rare in the cave-like interior of Eliphante. A window seat is accessed via a ledge, while all around built-in shelves and sculptural forms vie for attention. Stonework and mosaic, lit from above by reflective Mylar® painted in every hue, combine for an altar-like atmosphere.

The buildings are made of salvaged glass, ferrocement, and every imaginable kind of salvage. The photographer and writer on this project agree that looking at these images is challenging. There is little context for the forms Michael created, and his art was an effort to use everything, without letting anything dominate. "Michael knew a painting was done when no one color took precedence," Leda said. His architecture, likewise, marries many shapes and forms, each worthy of interest, but lost in the cacophony of the whole.

Skylights illuminate the tunnel entrance to the chamber inside Eliphante. Like many of the "discoveries" to be made on the four-acre installation, a passageway marks the transition to a new experience. Though it's basically a one-room building, it takes fifteen minutes to briefly explore the space, lending itself to disorientation. Seating in nooks and crannies, lofts and low spaces, allows those with time to sit and explore further.

Mesquite driftwood and river-formed rocks form complex mosaics in Michael's buildings. Smooth stucco walls were a canvas for his urge to paint.

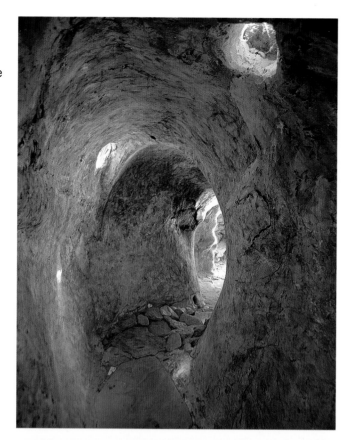

The couple lived in Leda's Winter Palace for seven years before Michael completed the Hippodome. This small shack is still her favorite building in the complex. It's where she sews and the library where she keeps her favorite books.

Tree stumps and driftwood mark the transition to yet another experience, a walk through the unique eco-climate hugging Oak Creek in the Arizona desert near Sedona.

Three rocks, carefully balanced, are typical of the discoveries to be made at Elephante.

In Arizona, life can be lived outdoors almost year round. An outdoor kitchen and dining pavilion is as much an artwork as a practical room. Michael built a wood-fired oven nearby, too, but Leda does much of her cooking in a solar oven they fashioned. "We didn't start out trying to be green, it just happened. We didn't have any money," she says. Of course, the couple was notorious among family members for "wasting" money on paint when they really needed food.

The Hippodome, where Leda and Michael lived together for over a decade, is a culmination of Michael's skills as a builder and architectural artist.

The entryway to the Hippodrome.

Michael Glastonbury, a British-born contractor who now lives in the Pacific Northwest, was camping around the United States with his wife in 1989 and "we met serendipitously," Leda said. "He stayed three months, and helped Michael." Glastonbury's artistic stamp is in the kitchen cabinets and countertop, where he let his artistic abilities run wild.

Mylar® adds a reflective flow from the ceiling and skylights on the living room of the Hippodome. Carpet mosaics were another of Michael's passions – he would cut and fit pieces of salvaged rug, some glued together, others just tightly wedged together to create his foot-friendly floors. Rock surrounds the deep soaking tub Michael fashioned in the middle of the room, while a blue, painted cloth covers a cushioned area flush with the rest of the floor.

The Mylar film that lines the Hippodome came in great big rolls shipped from New York City. "The Hippodome is built of rammed earth construction against the hillside, made of mud mixed with dried weeds and white glue packed into a form to create the Hippodome and Eliphante. There is some rebar and wire lathe, cement and, of course, paint. Michael painted everything," Leda said. She isn't boasting about Michael's skill as a builder, and worries about the future of Eliphante without an energetic caretaker like Michael. What's important about his work is that it is freeing. He made up his own definitions about what was important in a building, and in a life well lived.

The artificial turf that creates the otherworldly green for this Arizona installation was donated by the city of Cottonwood when they re-did their municipal tennis courts. It took the artists two years to distribute the carpet throughout the property. It helps, Leda says, in keeping the weeds and dust down, and it also helps her spot snakes when they are making their way around the site. Michael used some of the carpet to create an "Nennis Court," a place where they played ball without any lines or a net. Being adjacent to a creek, the area is lush anyway. If you're still, it's a garden alive with the buzz of bees and the constant movement of ants and little lizards. Pathways open through rock columns, caves, and driftwood arches, creating a sense of exploration.

A big step up from camping, the lifestyle of Leda Livant is a beautiful reminder of how simple life can be. A few pots and pans, a small assortment of dishes, and a limited wardrobe are adequate. It's art, creation, and experiences together that add up to happiness.

Incredible doorways offer an invitation
to explore at Eliphante.

"So many things were donated over the years," Leda said. "Most of what we built, we found here, just came from nature."

A nod the couple made to luxury is their solar heated bathhouse with a sunken tub. A hose feeds in solar heated water from a tank outside. Like every other building on the property, it's a giant mosaic of wood, rock, and paint.

Pipedreams is a semi-subterranean series of passageways Michael created. Cloth and foils form walls and add mystery as you make your way through a series of hallways that guide you through a chronological gallery of Michael's work, beginning in the 1960s and extending almost until his death in 2007. "Michael's paintings are not being cared for by the weather, or by the packrats," Leda said. "They can't stay here forever. It's the right artistic setting, but not the right physical setting. I'm looking for a home where fifteen major works can stay together."

Simplified Lifestyle

Rainbow Lonestar is an example of simplicity and contentment, both in her pleasant demeanor and spare abode. She delights in her life in an intentional community in Southwestern Virginia, and in the one-room straw-bale home she helped build with sweat and devotion.

Much of Rainbow's home was scrounged. The abundance of light that pours into her round home finds its way through windows that were free. There's only one new window in the building, one that someone bought but never used. Her big bank of picture windows that welcome the morning light were originally patio doors that were being thrown away. The front door was reclaimed, and had to be widened to fit the space.

A community effort, she began work on her home in October, preparing the foundation. This process took the better part of a year. Locust planks were salvaged from an old yurt platform nearby to form the sub-floor, a process that required a lot of labor hours, but cost nothing.

The framing was done in the spring. The straw bale walls, made with about 115 bales of local straw, went up in early summer and were plastered in July. The earthen plaster was a mix of lime, sand, and clay soil found on the land, mixed in small amounts using a wheelbarrow and hoe. There are two coats of plaster. To get the reddish brown inside, Rainbow mixed a clay slip with iron oxide stain and painted it on. The straw bale walls are about 18 inches thick and the plaster coating adds about a half inch or more to both the inside and outside. It took five people a weekend to plaster the house, taking shifts. Everyone on the job was self-taught.

Flame Bilyue, an artist from Charlottesville, created the mural on the outside. She spent hours embellishing the façade with river rock, bits of broken tile, and other treasured objects, so that each find their moment in the sun throughout the day to glitter or glow.

The metal roof would look perfectly round from above, but it is actually elliptical to create the slopes.

The home continues to save its owner money and support her easy maintenance lifestyle. Her highest electric bill was $10 one September because she ran a dehydrator for her tomatoes. It's hard to imagine how the fruits of a harvest could be stored in such a small structure, but as you'll see from the pictures, you can fit a lot of living in a small home.

A mural is part and parcel of the inch-thick plaster wall that coats the round straw-bale home in Southwestern Virginia.

A small wood bed constructed from reclaimed lumber. The forty-year-old stove keeps the home too warm – Rainbow rarely needs to use it, and often has to open a window in the winter.

A window illustrates the depth of the straw-bale walls, and is a favorite perch for beloved pet Shadow.

An altar of favorite things under windows formed from recycled patio doors displays gifts from friends and found objects with thoughts to contemplate. Wired for the Internet, a work center is home to paperwork, correspondence, and even a sound system.

The perfect fuel solution, this rack faces south for lots of air and sunshine for dry firewood. A roof slanted toward the north fends off most rain.

The Contractor's Home

Paul Lacinski used to design and build straw bale houses for a living. "I built about a hundred of them," he said. He was busy building them when he and his partner, Amy Klippenstein, set out to build their studio in 1999, which is why they worked on theirs during the non-traditional winter months. And it took about three years to finish.

And it's finished. "We've done a lot of drawings and tried this and there is no good way to add on to it, to build an addition." Paul said. "The fact that we can't gracefully expand it has kept us from doing anything stupid," he laughs.

The small house is round, Paul said, "because that's what the site wanted. We did a bunch of different sketches of different possibilities and it was just the one that fit best here. Their lot is limited in size, with severe drop offs that limit the footprint of the home.

The round design appealed to Paul on two levels: he's always had a fascination with yurts, ("real yurts, not geeky wooden imitations") and incorporated some yurt features into his home. "Plus we'd never built anything round, so we were interested in trying it."

Paul said that both he and Amy "have a rather intense dislike of octagons." So they built round, even though it meant far more challenge in the building process. "The fact that it's round drastically complicated everything. There was never a 90-degree cut on anything –the floorboards, the kitchen counters, anything," he said. One concession was the roof, which was easiest to frame out in an octagon shape. "That's actually why we ended up with a living roof. We were going to do slate, but that would accentuate the octagon shape."

The roof has the same rubber membrane used on all flat roofs, plus a couple inches of soil, "and whatever happened to grow out of it. It's a weed roof."

The house stays cool under that natural sod all summer, with the exceptions of some mid-day hot spots created by a skylight. In the winter they require only about a cord of wood to heat the place, making fires only once or twice a day. "It's hard to say because we've never had any really good hardwood; we usually burn junky clean up wood."

Amy and Paul live much of their life outdoors. Amy co-founded a farmer's market in Ashfield and they make their living together as organic farmers – selling fresh produce in the summer and milking ten cows year round to sell milk and yogurt.

This petite straw bale home seems to have mushroomed on site by itself. It is sheltered here by snow that blankets the sod roof. Heating is quick work for a small woodstove inside, and the summer heat has little effect through both the dense canopy of hemlock and pine in this wooded site.

Appliances and limited cabinetry enjoy wall space under picture windows in the one-room studio. Curtains help conceal some storage. In such a small living space, clutter is "mandatory," Paul said. "A bigger house has more capacity to absorb disorder. A very small mess in a small house feels like a lot of mess." So, whereas those cleanup jobs in bigger homes can seem monumental, Paul says he enjoys his low-maintenance job. "We spend ten minutes picking up at the end of each day. Pretty much nothing sticks around that isn't really necessary. It's nice not to have a lot of extraneous junk lying around. I like that."

Two nearby sheds help with the seldom-used possessions. Inside a closet holds off-season clothes, extra kitchen appliances, extra paper for the ink-jet printer, etc. The front of the "purple door shed" is straw bale, Paul said. He used it as a hands-on project for a class he taught in straw bale construction, and left the one wall up at the request of his students, who'd grown attached.

Despite their fervent attempts to hide the shape of the octagonal roof, the skylight "is where the octagonal nature reveals itself," Paul said. The light has five clear panels that illuminate the interior, and three that are insulated panels. The three that are covered are a lesson learned from yurt kits that have a plastic dome on top, Paul said. "They are nice by day, they let sun in. But at night the light shoots up from below like a shaft of light and we weren't crazy about that."

Using a hardware kit bought from Create-A-Bed®, they fashioned their own fold-up Murphy bed. "It's a lot easier. You don't really have to make your bed. You sort of tuck in the sheets and you stick the pillows under the elastic strap. It takes somewhere between five and ten seconds."

The owners actually ended switching to a smaller woodstove as their first cast-iron heater could quickly turn the room into a sauna. Paul describes stoking up the heater with hardwood to keep the place warm while they were gone, and coming home to find that candles were "bent over." Behind the stove, apple cider ferments.

A neighbor, Bob Markey, loaned a sculpture of metal, concrete, and tile mosaic to adorn the property.

Expanding Design

Chris Rawlings called on his friend Paul Lacinsky when it came time to build his own straw bale house, but he takes sole credit for the design. Both graduates of the Rhode Island School of Design, Chris admits that his wife is every bit as talented in the creative department as he. Then he laughs as he describes seeking her input on the location of the bathroom as she was nursing the first of two daughters and learning a lesson in immediate priorities.

The couple broke ground for the home in 2000 and did everything themselves with the help of friends. It will never be done, though, he said, as changes are constant. "I'm still building it and will be for the rest of my life," he said. There have been two additions to the original 1,164 square foot home – a sunroom and 900 square feet of additional bedroom space. Next up are plans to add an addition and move the kitchen. And there's always a need for more closet space, Chris said,

marveling at the mess two young daughters can make.

Key to the home's energy efficient and passive solar nature are walls of well-placed windows and thermal mass in the concrete floor and the thick plaster on the straw bale walls. The house stays cool in summer, warm at night, but because of its nature, it doesn't follow the cycles of the year, Chris said. He has to make more adjustments during the in-between spring and fall seasons with his central woodstove.

Lots of windows admit sunlight and warmth to the Rawling home. They bought Pella windows from a seconds store, where most of the windows were never actually installed. The couple added their own artistic stamp, painting one mural of windows to create a mosaic and using like primary tones on the roof supports.

A corner is composed of a mix of windows, aligned in a mosaic, which floods the living area with light.

An antique dresser creates dichotomy in the otherwise contemporary setting, and helps define a space. It's mass also acts as a sound buffer in the open room.

The dining area, likewise, is situated in a panoramic setting, looking out through the newly added greenhouse. The lighting was designed by James Deter, "the best man at my wedding, who has dform.com in Brooklyn," Chris said. "This was the prototype of a set he made for a restaurant in Chicago."

The central woodstove provides heat for the entire home. The blue wall beyond is a bathroom.

An open shower is in keeping with the exposed plumbing that illustrates the open nature, and heart, of the designer.

To Gnome is to Love Him

"Ho mi takoda" means welcome, and Humphreys' home has this message posted for all who approach. He has exchanged the greeting with well over a hundred thousand visitors.

The home of Richard Humphreys and his wife, Linda, is as much about the surrounding property as it is the rambling home. The home is anchored by its original stone structure, built more than 200 years ago. It's unclear when the first log section was built, but it is made of American Chestnut, which is now extinct, so it's well over 100 years old. Richard bought the property in 1976, and as his family grew (with two sons and a daughter), he needed to add on. He purchased an antique log cabin ten miles away, moved it to his site, and hired Amish craftsmen to help put the addition together.

From that storied past, Rich has expanded his home into the wooded acres beyond, and brought wooded treasures in. His home embodies the best of the forest to be found in Eastern Pennsylvania. "The inside was more the doing of my wife, I spend most of my time outside," Humphreys said. In fact, he credits fifty years of survival with Type 1 diabetes to the endless labor on his land — a labor of love.

"I love to stack rocks," he says. He gathers up the stones his Amish neighbors cast aside as they clear their fields for planting, and he finds new homes for them in his extensive network of stonewalls and stacked sculptures. In addition, he mulches paths and keeps his trees free of strangling vines.

Humphreys' mission has been melding lore of the woodland's little people with lessons about Nature's rich treasures. The former public school art teacher now gives his lessons here, at Gnome Countryside nestled in the rolling hills of Lancaster County. He brings children, and adults, into his realm of delight, where they enjoy fireside stories of "little gnome facts," woodland walks, building gnome houses, and activities like stone stacking and drumming to help them reconnect with wonder and their ability to delight in it.

"The idea came about because of two reasons," Humphreys relates: "One was spending time in Denmark and being enchanted by the sincere and child-like belief the older folks there have in the little people. Also, when I taught elementary art, I would occasionally use elves as a motivational technique for some of my art lessons. When I did, I could see the children transported from one place to another."

He now has up to 6,000 children a year pass through his program. He uses stories about the little people who inhabit the forest to launch lessons on environmental awareness and respect, with lessons in zoology, geology, biology, and native plant identification. More information about his educational programs is available at www.gnomecountryside. com.

An exploration of Rich's work would be lacking without exploring both inside and out. We hope you enjoy this tour of the "gnome biome" as much as we did.

The original stone home Richard
Humphreys bought in the late 1970s
has been expanded twice. Once when
a matching log structure was added on
at least 100 years ago. Again when the
growing Humphreys family acquired
another log home from nearby and
moved it to the site with the help of an
Amish crew.

A caretaker of the forest around him, Rich says that removing the wild grapevines is a favor to the trees. The vines were recycled here, used to adorn a porch along with natural garland that lends color to a mid-winter landscape.

Rich handcrafted the whimsical siding that frames the back of his home, and the entry beyond the home to his magical wooded play land. The boy climbing a tree reflects his own passion for climbing trees. Inspired by naturalist John Muir's memoirs about riding a tree through a storm, Rich has done the same, and his story is one of many inspirational tales this Type 1 diabetes survivor of fifty-plus years shares with his students. He still finds time to spend high among the limbs, and advocates for the experience. "My wife and I just love to climb trees."

One addition to the property includes a sauna, fancifully constructed with a Swedish-inspired roofline and colorful trim. The sauna is heated by a wood fire with quartz and ironstone atop a stainless steel barrel, housed in the stone vault on the side of the building. The building design was inspired by a friend's sketch, and the interior was carefully excavated into a hillside. An antechamber was fashioned around exposed bedrock – a cool neighbor after a hot session on the sauna room.

Opposite page:
A coal stove helps to heat the home, and to cook the food in the sprawling kitchen. The slate capping the stone wall behind and above the stove came from an old barn roof, as did the antique weathervane. The #2 pine plank floor in the kitchen is "the cheapest floor you can do," Humphreys points out, though he dressed it up with walnut pegs. Leftover chestnut logs from the antique log addition were milled to make the chestnut cabinets in the kitchen. A corner countertop was created using a checkerboard of wood and Corian®.

Stacking rocks find their way into this home, as well as adorning the entire property. These playthings fill the sill in a breakfast nook off the kitchen, overlooking Rich's wooded wonderland beyond. "I just love to stack stone," Humphreys says. His property is peppered with stone stacks as art, and walls crisscross his hillside in testament to his constant work/create ethic. Humphreys credits his fifty-plus years of type one diabetes survival to exercise and constant diligence. His Amish neighbors pile rocks on the edge of their tilled fields, and Humphreys happily provides a removal service.

Not surprisingly, Rich raised three children with an artistic bent. His daughter, Courtney, is responsible for the mirror mosaic work in the upstairs bath.

Inspired by a store display in Ohio, Rich came home determined to create an indoor pond of his own. This indoor oasis was created using stone found on the property. The fireplace, on the other hand, was inspired by a trip to the Southwest. Once heated, the entire solid-stone mass mortared over with cement warms up and helps heat the home.

The exposed exterior of the old log home provides a beautiful indoor wall. Bits of the outdoors make it inside.

Outside, a niche in the butt and pass log home offers a treat for one inquisitive enough to go seeking.

An archway is created by locust root harvested from windfall.

Stones inspire throughout the property, this one quite literally.

A thinking spot.

An enormous drum sits in the center of a hilltop gazebo. Visitors are encouraged to express themselves from this inspiring vantage.

The original barn provides a non-descript shell for an artistic life lived within and without. The garden lies dormant in winter, but a greenhouse room is lush with life for a couple that loves the outdoors. A second-floor deck was crafted to preserve a tree. An arbor in the back is a favorite summer spot.

Dave and Alice call their home "Amish Mod" style. They took a concrete block home that was initially built by a young Amish couple. A starter house, it served as barn, home, and laundry to the original owners. Dave and Alice likewise use it for animals – they have nine cats

that wander in and out, and they have been adding their own touch to the various spaces since moving in and calling it home in 1990.

A cabinetmaker by trade, Dave has adorned the doors with his custom molding. Both are artists, and the house is chock-a-block full of Alice's paintings and Dave's exquisite woodwork.

They call their home "The Island." It serves as an escape for many friends, who come there to feel rejuvenated. "People come here and they just relax, they feel like they get away from everything," Alice said.

A custom door and a handmade frame reflect Dave's work. The painted wall panel was done by a good friend, Terry Sourbeer Redcrow.

Dovetailed joinery in door surrounds display Dave's warm touch. A mirror, likewise, displays his attention to detail. The vanity in the guest bath was crafted to include found wood from the property and to reflect a reverence for nature. Alice's paintings are displayed side-by side with Dave's collection of Native American objects and inspired wood art.

Dave repeats a tree motif throughout the home, crafting faux transoms with carved wood and glass.

The stair banister was crafted from recycled materials: the rail came from an old bed frame, antlers form braces, and the newel post is an old vine.

Self-made Soak

Thomas Fetterman has been too busy traveling the world for fun, and finding ways to make life more livable for handicapped people, to do a lot of building on his home. However, when it came to his love of a deep soak, he made his own tub perfect for his daily practice. It was important to us to include him in this book – because of him we gained access to several other homes in his unique, intentional community of Bryn Gweled.

Who says you have to buy a fancy tub? Thomas Fetterman created his own, working with a wood frame and applying wire, concrete, and tile. He modeled his design after a Japanese soaking tub. He spends about two hours a day soaking, doing his reading, and thinking.

Block House

The original house was very small when the Bob and Louise Kidder bought their home in 1972. They looked to architect Bob Bishop to help them enlarge the structure to more comfortably accommodate a growing family. Bishop, a student of Frank Lloyd Wright, had designed many of the homes in the Bryn Gweled intentional community, established in 1940 near Philadelphia. He sketched out ideas and developed blueprints for the Kidders, who did the work themselves.

The original home was designed with four parallel cinder block walls, with a framed wall of glass between each. The new plan included a clerestory area over the kitchen, which the Kidders accomplished by taking a circular saw to the roof and then jacking up the whole thing from below, allowing them to build the windows. Douglas fir beams were installed.

They then added two bedrooms, a second bathroom, and a family room, accomplishing all this work while their son was an infant and both were working to achieve tenure on the faculty at Temple University.

Bluestone floor was added to the family room and tile floor in the living room, topping a water-fed subfloor heating system. The hot water system wasn't put to use for fifteen years, however, because the complex solar system designed for the home made it unnecessary. However, while the Kidders lived in Japan for four years, the solar heating system was misused and destroyed by tenants.

Heating hadn't been a big concern when the Kidders began their renovation of the house. "We completed the project literally four months before the oil embargo," Bob says. "Oil was so cheap before that, and no one was thinking about the cost of fuel oil."

The clerestory design is perfect in the summer, with two vent windows that allow hot air to escape and vent windows in the front wall of windows that feed in cool air. Moreover, they close the blinds to block summer sun. They've never needed air conditioning.

Trelliswork creates an open, architectural feel to the front of the Kidder's cinderblock home while admitting sunlight to warm the home in the winter. The red and black finish and natural stonework help add to the Asian aura the Kidder's home embodies. They spent five years abroad in Japan, and their home is a showcase for treasures brought back from abroad.

Inside, the front wall of the home is completely open, flanked by sturdy concrete block walls. Lower windows in the front crank open to admit cool air in the summer, while clerestory windows in the next room open to vent out warm air.

The addition of a clerestory over the kitchen provided natural ventilation for the home.

Louise crafted the copper colored tiles on the backsplash with their leaf imprints and painted the chair in the dining room.

The Kidders fashioned shelves and a post in their home from recycled organ pipes. The organ wood dates back to 1870 or so, and is incredible knot-free old growth pine. What wasn't kept intact was used as paneling over the sliding doors in the new addition. The pipple, or angled board that creates the organ's sound, was preserved on some of the shelves, for their novelty and beauty. It was very noisy, the Kidders laugh, when they transported the whistling pipes atop their car from the pipes' original home in an upstate New York church.

The Kidder's designed their bathroom floor mosaic, inspired by their travels in Japan and Bali, and crafted it from polished stones.

Growing Standards

The home of Ed Kramer and Beth Hartman Kramer, northeast of Philadelphia, is a study in the expanding notion of what a "simple" house is. Originally a simple glass block on the hill, set on a slab, each successive owner has felt the need to expand. The Kramer's undertook a major rebuild after buying this house in the intentional community of Bryn Gweled in 1986.

At its heart, the home is a big open room with character posts of unmilled cypress supporting the beams. Subsequent additions created a much larger footprint, albeit small by many modern home standards, with a wonderful atrium standing at the center of the home.

A small house has grown with the families that occupied it.

Un-milled cypress posts support the living and family room areas of the home, which act as open galleries to display art by Ed and Beth.

An open area at the center of the home acts as an atrium. The atrium: "It's so nice to see snow in here in the winter," Beth said. "We built snowmen in there when the kids were little."

Ed took one woodworking course before taking on this ambitious master bedroom project. His custom cabinetry includes a drop-ceiling canopy over the bed to make it warmer and built-ins that keep the intimate space clutter free. Like his paintings (see www. kramerart.net), his woodworking plays with linear lines and patterns.

Meditation Creation

The home is small, but it's been subdivided: the living room has two levels, with a children's play area above the sitting area, reached by a ladder. He has a basketball hoop inside, and grandchildren are allowed to throw balls in the house!

Peter Rhodes and his wife Roxanne have called their Bryn Athyn house home for over thirty years. Given his druthers, however, Peter will be outside putting pieces of this and that together for whimsical sculptures that dot his lawn, or they will both be at peace in their individual meditation huts on the property. Peter even works as close to the outdoors as possible, conducting his counseling program in a small backyard room that feels more like a porch.

He has written books on spiritual growth, though it's hard to imagine him spending time typing. It's hard to keep him inside his house, or even home. His favorite place is a local barn where donated items are sold to benefit local charities. Rhodes helps sort through all the incoming, and takes bits many would cast aside and finds new life for them in his art. The resale shop is full of his treasures, but his home even more so. The grounds around his home are

literally littered with found treasure and repurposed art, much of it noise or motion producing.

Rhodes leads a joyful tour around his wooded compound, allowing us to explore the meditation and counseling centers he has crafted. No path passes quickly, however, as a million pauses are offered by the sculptures and objects that vie for attention, or contemplation.

A mantel is the last remnant of a barn that once stood on the property.

A plank bridges a small stream and provides access to a two-story meditation tower Peter built for his wife, a practicing yogi.

Peter's personal meditation chamber is miniscule. He has a heater inside set on a timer so that he can use the hut year round.

His beloved meditation
sessions wouldn't be complete
without a dip in the pond, the
colder the better!

Rhodes built this counseling room, like most everything else on the property, from salvaged items. He finds his happiness in creating. He's the kind of counselor, he says, who asks his clients "why do you like to feel unhappy?"

The grounds are full of whimsical objects and Peter's self-taught art. He volunteers at a the Red Barn Gift Shop, a benefit thrift shop where he is a major customer for donated items that fuel his addiction to creating. Many of his sculptures make noise, like a bell set within a circle fashioned for stacking wood. A series of sculptures are flanked by organ speakers on either side that can be aimed to amplify the noise. The neighbors remain on good terms!

Spanish Influence

In creating *Lautra Place* (The Other Place), a studio workshop behind her Arts & Crafts era Pasadena home, Maurine St. Gaudens and her friend/contractor plotted each detail carefully.

"When my friend, John Dunn, and I decided to build the studio, we wanted to keep it consistent with the house, which is Arts and Crafts, but I also wanted to use my imagination, and my taste, which is more Tudor and Spanish." Her home is within walking distance of downtown Pasadena, California, so Maurine was dealing with pure Arts & Crafts aesthetics. She was also bringing her more Gothic taste to the project, and a collector's acquisitive nature. In other words, she scrounged up many of the wonderful parts that went into the building. For starters, she turned her collection of windows into an architectural mosaic.

"I've always collected doors and windows. I love doors and windows, and you never know where you can pop one in. I collect doors and windows with personalities. Some of the windows in the building are eighteenth century. I love the old, rippled glass."

That free rein for creativity was part of the design process. We worked from sketches we did each night. Every night we'd sit down and figure out what the next step was.

Not that it was that unplanned. The building was constructed on a floating platform so that it can ride out any earthquake. It can also be easily detached and moved. Moreover, it was carefully fitted to a footprint that didn't disturb any of the existing trees.

Because she uses the building as an art restoration studio, light was very important. The windows serve a great purpose there, and colored glass was not incorporated in order to avoid light refraction that might alter the artwork inside. Moreover, the setting was created with Maurine's art lamps in mind, as a perfect setting for showing off the artisan light sculptures that Maurine creates with her business partner, Tracy Chamberlin. These unique lamps are fashioned in Arts & Crafts style "somewhere between the architect Gaudi and Goth" and made of mica, copper, and bronze.

Opposite page:
The story of *Lautra Place* is one that is equal parts craft and recovery. The building is full of delightful windows, lighting, and architectural elements that were being cast aside for new development and found a new home with a woman who specializes in art restoration.

A wide veranda was incorporated for *Lautra Place* for entertaining. "The decks are extremely wide because we wanted to be able to move big furniture out there and have parties. The porch rail is ultra wide so that you can put plates and glasses on it. The support posts are all period posts and the railings go around them so that we didn't have to alter them at all. "The window ledges are deep so that they act as ledges, so people can put their drinks there. But they are flush inside because I don't want any fluids in there," Maurine said. "I wanted to do something different with windows."

Opposite page:
"Each window is different, and every windowsill is different – each has its own motif."

It pays to have friends in the art world. Maurine got one friend to custom-make the redwood shingles to replicate tree bark. Even the paint was specially mixed by a friend – the orange color to match the tangelo tree next to it, and the dark color "created to look like little animal fur."

One of Maurine's favorite stories is the history of two arch-topped French doors that now provide different views into and from *Lautra Place*. "They were given to me probably twenty-five to thirty years ago. We weren't going to use them for anything, so we gave them to a friend. He gave them to a friend who took them to Utah, and when we started the work that friend sent them back to me. I was so happy to have my doors back."

Opposite page:
Colored glass didn't have to be altogether shunned. This incredible window found a place as a hanging art piece on the front veranda.

The top of the deck rail was fashioned extra wide, wide enough to support a dinner plate. The railing was fashioned to encircle historic posts without touching them.

A collection of antique lighting, much of it from Maurine's beloved Spanish roots, is displayed inside and out at *Lautra Place*.

Rare art and a lifetime of antique
collection are displayed in *Lautra
Place*. "The beams, which are very
real, came from an 1870s hospital
in Los Angeles," Maurine said. The
salvaged beams were 18 feet long 6 x
8 clear grain redwood, she said. "We
were able to take those, split them in
half to keep the original patina, and
embed them in the walls. We were
very lucky to find the architectural
pieces," she adds. How could anyone
disagree?

"The corbels are eighteenth century polychromed Spanish corbels. They were not cut, either, but the wall was cut to accommodate them."

"I wanted the walls to have personality. I had a friend do the plaster. None of the walls are flat – they all undulate and they are soft like a baby's skin. The walls are all 8 inches thick, so it stays so cool so beautifully."

Lautra Place was designed as a photo studio to create settings for photographing Maurine's artwork. It is designed for photographing the "lighting sculptures" that Maurine creates with business partner Tracy Chamberlin. "We make mica do things it doesn't like to do," Maurine says, describing how they use heat to bend and sometimes scorch the mica to create the look they want.

Like mother, like son. Roger Kintz built an artist's cottage behind his Eagle Rock home in suburban Los Angeles using salvaged treasures. In his case, a wealth of stained glass windows recycled from a church in Riverside City add beauty to the home, fill it with light, and protect the privacy of the renter who lives within. Antique Arts & Crafts era and Spanish lighting illuminates indoors and out, and a parquet floor was rescued from a defunct Italian restaurant in Pasadena. The rough sawn lumber that frames out the house was gleaned from an old fence business. The paints were all non-toxic, and the woods were sealed with linseed oil to keep the environment healthy.

The most special feature, though, is the Pentagonal roof, where five points come together and create what Roger describes as an energy that's "almost like a vortex. Anyone who sleeps up in that loft sleeps very deeply. It's very pleasant, very high energy," he said. "It was an unintentional byproduct of the design," he adds.

The design was the result of Roger's strict insistence that none of the trees be harmed, that no branch be cut. So the steep roof and small footprint were carefully inserted onto the 10,000 square foot lot behind his existing house.

Bright, cheerful colors and a collection of pretty windows, all artfully framed, give this Artist's Cottage its dollhouse feeling.

Antique lighting outdoors comes from
two inspirations: 1. Roger's mother
shared her gene for collecting and
displaying such treasures, and 2.
California's wonderful climate helps
preserve the pieces.

Opposite page:
A ladder from a telephone company
switching room was repurposed
to provide loft access. Roger had
hardware designed that allows the
ladder to be tucked flat against the
wall to save floor space when not
in use, and to angle out and lock in
place when someone is climbing up or
down.

After ten years working as a landscape architect in Massachusetts and California, Andy Mueller found a new calling in designing and building natural homes. His company, GreenSpace Collaborative Design & Build in Charlemont, Massachusetts, keeps him busy at his designing desk all winter, and on-site building homes throughout New England every summer. Luckily, the efficient, well insulated, and low maintenance straw bale home he built for himself requires little work from him to heat and maintain.

Despite the cold winter and hot summer temperature swings of the New England climate, the home's heating loads require a cord of wood for heating during the winter months and no air cooling in the summer due to the thermal mass of the straw bale and plaster walls. He uses propane as supplementary heat when he is gone for any length of time, and to heat his hot water and fire up his stove. Still, he only has to fill his 320-gallon propane tank about every three years. And electricity averages $30 a month. So he figures he's spending $1.05 a day for heat and electricity combined throughout the year.

The building of his 1,000-square foot home commenced in the summer of 2000 using approximately 250 bales of two-string straw. And despite the old adage about a cobbler's children never having shoes, he completely finished construction of the house over that winter. "Having a full-time job and building this house was a true test of mental and physical fortitude,"

he said. In fact, he'd planned it as an in-law suite and was going to build a larger home on the property elsewhere with his partner. "This was going to be the practice house, but we decided to live here after realizing how involved being a homeowner/builder can be." They ultimately decided that the effort of building another wasn't a priority, so they modified their floor plan to accommodate their lifestyle.

The straw bale home has a lime plaster finish and a high R rating. In other words, it's insulated to an R-value of 27 to 30 "as opposed to the conventional R-19 that most builders install in homes today." The roof has enough blown cellulose under its aluminum cap to give it an R-49 value. "I believe the roof is one of the most important parts of the house to insulate against heat transfer. A lot of heat is lost through

roofs. So we paid close attention to that." Andy said.

"It's a passive solar design with a concrete slab floor that stores daily heat during the winter months," he said. "In the summer, the sun never penetrates the thermal mass of the walls and the concrete floors keep it cool. I don't require air conditioning."

"This is however more difficult to do on a larger scale – 1,000 feet seems to work very well for us," he said.

Besides remarkably low heating costs, and non-existent cooling costs, Andy is proud of the fact that his home was built using local resources and lots of salvaged, re-purposed materials.

Although his masters degree from the University of Massachusetts in Amherst is in landscape architecture, Andy learned natural building design through a sense of his own

A red lime-plaster finish is the distinguishing feature of this straw bale home. The thickness of the walls and the incredible insulation of the home make it remarkably efficient.

curiosity and investigation. He also learned a lot, though, from ten years of working in conjunction with architects, designers, and engineers, seeing how they did their jobs. "I've gained a lot of practical experience from them.

Andy made his own concrete countertops, "before the wave of popularity for concrete countertops," he said. He also designed the open floor plan using a non-traditional post and beam framing system. "We used metal fasteners, a very quick, inexpensive, and easy way to erect a frame with two people. And it was a fraction of the cost of a traditional timber frame."

This small woodstove was centrally located in the home and, together with an industrial house fan to circulate the heat, it warms the entire home very efficiently. Reclaimed windows on the back wall louver out to allow heat to circulate into the bathroom above.

Andy liked the idea of all the materials being
"basically raw in form." The concrete floor,
in particular, draws a lot of comments. The
joints were hand-tooled to make them look
like large tiles. He applied a clear sealant on
the floor that brought out the natural, mottled
color of the concrete.

Corrugated steel salvaged from old elevator shafts make stylish room dividers in the home.

Andy designed his own railing systems. The stair rail uses steel cables with turnbuckles.

A living area downstairs is a study in disciplined living. Having a small footprint for the home involved leaving the space very open, without a lot of built-ins for storage.

"This addition was basically a need for privacy," Andy said of the upstairs bedroom. We needed a room where we could get away when there were guests staying downstairs. It's amazing what a difference it makes.

A bump-out dormer was a later addition that added a lot of living space, Andy said. Reclaimed windows act as a railing, and the mass of windows help reflect sound back downstairs to make the loft area quieter. This is where Andy works when he's home, planning designs for other people's natural homes. The corrugated steel dividers were not cut floor to ceiling on purpose, he said. "I cut them off at 6 feet to allow natural convection. Otherwise I would have to put a secondary heating system upstairs and that just didn't make sense."

Author's Endnote

I hope these images have inspired you to leave your own mark on a home that expresses who you are and what you can do. Freedom doesn't just mean the ability to buy whatever you want and to make as much money as you can. Freedom means the ability to be who you are. Part of discovering and expressing yourself is the clothing you wear and the house you inhabit. Try on different shells! Freedom is living in a home that fulfills you personally, meeting your comfort requirements, and not necessarily the dictates of standard building codes written by industry lobbyists.

Hopefully this book is just another in a long tradition of celebratory publications. We'll be looking for more unusual houses to photograph, and I'd love to hear from you about your home, or another admirable structure you know of. Feel free to contact me at tinas@schifferbooks.com.